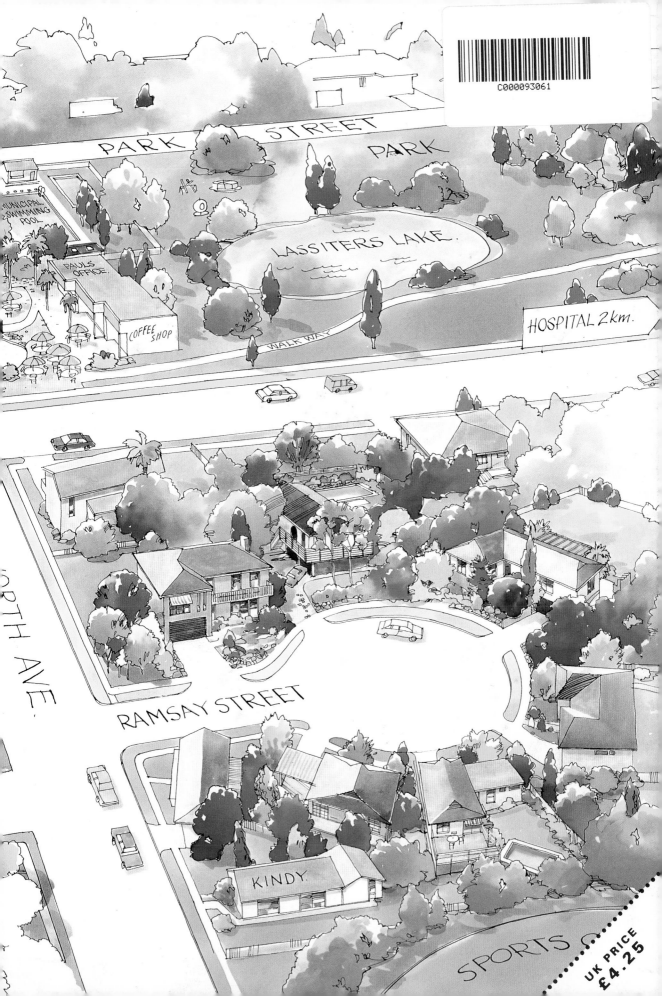

1992
Neighbours™
THE OFFICIAL ANNUAL

Ian Morrison

HAMLYN

CONTENTS

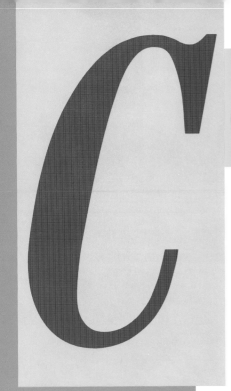

Photographic acknowledgements
All photographs reproduced in this book were supplied by Grundy Television Pty Ltd except for the following: *Australian Overseas Information Service, London* 20, 21, 38, 39, 44, 45, 54, 55; *Rex Features* 28, 29.

Published in 1991
by The Hamlyn Publishing Group Limited
part of Reed International Books
Michelin House, 81 Fulham Road,
London SW3 6RB

ISBN 0 600 57311 7

Printed in Great Britain

Designed by Maggie Aldred

1992

Since *Neighbours* was first seen in Britain in October 1986 there are many fans who have seen every one of the one thousand-plus episodes. And many even watch both showings each day! That's over 2,500 times that they have shared in the trials and tribulations of the residents of Ramsay Street.

Many videos are set in the morning for the lunch-time broadcast so kids can take up position in front of the TV when they come home from school at four o'clock. And less than two hours later they watch the same episode again. That's the appeal of *Neighbours*.

The episodes bring their share of dramas, heartaches and sadness. But we also share those brighter moments in the Erinsborough sunshine of our *Neighbours* more than 10,000 miles away. And many of us feel as though we know the likes of Madge Bishop, Jim Robinson, and Des Clarke as much, if not more, than our own neighbours.

INTRODUCTION

When the characters have problems, we feel as though we are sharing them. We sympathise when things go wrong, like Des and Paul being unlucky in love or Harold's dogged attempts to put the world to rights. And how we empathise with Helen; she tries so hard to make everybody else's life run as smoothly as possible.

Residents may come and go from Ramsay Street, but the most famous street in Melbourne never changes. It is that one place that rules our lives twice a day for five days of the week. And such is the pulling power that it not only stays top of the ratings but, at the start of the Gulf War in January 1991, when many programmes were taken off the air, Neighbours, while re-scheduled occasionally, never lost a single episode — a testament indeed to the popularity of Australia's top drama serial. Even wars can't stop Neighbours!

HAPPY DAYS AT Erinsborough

Like it or not, the kids of Ramsay Street have eventually to go to school, and when they reach the age of 12 it is off to Erinsborough High.

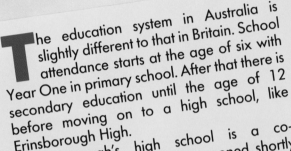

The education system in Australia is slightly different to that in Britain. School attendance starts at the age of six with Year One in primary school. After that there is secondary education until the age of 12 before moving on to a high school, like Erinsborough High.

Erinsborough's high school is a co-educational school and was opened shortly after the last war and many of the parents of today's younger *Neighbours* residents attended the school before their offspring.

Headmaster Mr Muir had some difficult situations to encounter; the most recent of which was the sit-in in the common room instigated by Matt, Sharon and Nick.

The acting principal, Mr Payne, also had his problems. It was during his reign as Erinsborough High's head that Josh hacked into the computer and changed Todd's examination grades to 'A'. But it backfired on Josh because, as a result of such good marks Todd was chosen for the school's quiz team. However, after changing the results back to their more realistic marks, Josh was himself selected for the team.

Head teachers are rarely popular and when Dorothy Burke arrived to take over as Erinsborough High's new principal she soon found out how *not* to win over the pupil's affections when one of her first duties was to segregate the boys and girls for some lessons. This didn't go down well with the pupils. And when Dorothy introduced a new music appreciation session it was greeted with groans from the pupils. But their groans turned into delight when they found out that they had to appreciate one of Australia's top bands, *Go 101*.

High

LAUGH

'The subjects I enjoyed most were maths and . . . lunch time.'
Kristian Schmid

Cody Willis (Amelia Frid) is one of the newcomers to Erinsborough High. She is seen (far left) in her uniform, (above) relaxing with Todd (Kristian Schmid) and (top) studying with Todd. (Left) Keeping a watchful eye over Erinsborough pupils is headmistress Dorothy Burke (Maggie Dence).

M̲elanie...does

Melanie . . . she's the one with that amazing laugh. And Lucinda Cowden admits it is the question most asked of her when stopped in the street: 'Do you really laugh like that?' Happily she can honestly answer 'No'.

Lucinda reckons she is dissimilar to Melanie, although she is fun in real life, just like her character. It was that fun aspect which attracted her to the role. Mind you, if she could play another character in *Neighbours* she would like to play Harold!

Lucinda was born at Ballarat and went to school in Melbourne. English, drama and dance were her favourite subjects and, for someone who plays the part of a secretary, she failed typing and short-hand at school.

Now feeling secure following her success in the series she would like to return to theatre acting one day and, hopefully, appear in a feature film.

In her precious spare time Lucinda enjoys the outdoor life and can be seen horse riding or water skiing. She is a bit of a sports nut and enjoys watching football (the Aussie Rules variety) on the television and enjoys a day watching cricket, no doubt packed up with pasta and some Long Island Iced Tea . . . her idea of a good 'bagging'. She is certainly not one for the high-heeled shoes and blue eyeshadow which she says are two of her pet hates.

Lucinda lives in a single-fronted house in Melbourne, which she describes as 'falling down'. And of *her* own neighbours she says: 'They're fabulous'.

she help or hinder?

Lucinda Cowden

'For privacy, I take my holidays anywhere that Neighbours isn't shown.'

Ben Geurens

'The most appealing part about playing Toby is all the mischief he gets up to.'

# of Ramsay Street

Miranda Fryer and Ben Geurens are two of the youngest members of the Neighbours cast, but they seem to be coping with their success.

Miranda Fryer

Both Miranda Fryer and Ben Geurens were born in Melbourne and attend school in the city. Ben goes to the Pinewood Primary, while Miranda attends the Summerhill Park Kindergarten.

Miranda was 'discovered' for her part in *Neighbours* when spotted in a local supermarket, while Ben set his heart on an acting career from an early age and attended a drama workshop at Monash University. He was good at stunts and doubled for Lochy McLachlan (Amber Kilpatrick) before landing the part of Toby.

Miranda's favourite reading material is *Thomas the Tank Engine* while Ben enjoys Roald Dahl and Paul Jonnings. When it comes to eating, Ben likes good old fashioned English fish-and-chips, accompanied by a glass of 'lemo', while Miranda is happy with a bag of crisps.

Most of the *Neighbours* cast seem to own cats as pets and Miranda and Ben are no exception. Miranda has three: Phoebe, Richard and Trafalgar. Ben's cat is called simply 'Puss' and is good company for his Alsatian dog 'Crystal'.

Miranda can be stubborn and temperamental, just like Skye, and when it comes to wearing clothes her favourites are 'anything apart from what my mum *wants* me to wear'. Perhaps predictably, one of her pet hates is 'being told what to do' . . . according to her mum!

Ben knows what his favourite clothes are, and *he* chooses them . . . quicksilver shorts and tank tops. He is also positive about his future plans because: 'When I grow up I want to be a surgeon *and* a sportsman.'

Matt Robinson

Matt certainly isn't a mummy's boy, but Hilary would have liked to have taken complete control of his life.

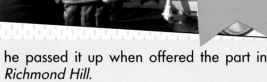

When Matt Robinson first appeared in Ramsay Street, he came as a fresh-faced 17-year-old. But in reality, Ashley Paske is two years older than the character he plays.

Before he joined *Neighbours* Ashley had plenty of television experience, including a year playing Marty in *Richmond Hill*, another Grundy production.

Ashley doesn't like watching television, but enjoys the cinema and particularly likes Richard Dreyfuss movies. He was born at Nowra, New South Wales. His mother was English and his father German. Understandably, Ashley was good at German in high school and had a chance to go on a three-month scholarship to Germany, but he passed it up when offered the part in *Richmond Hill*.

There are similarities between Matt's life and Ashley's. Both have had to cope with their parents splitting up; Ashley's did so when he was young. Matt and Ashley had to adapt to new homes; Matt doing so when he moved to Ramsay Street and Ashley when he had to move from Wollongong to settle in Melbourne for the series.

While Ashley's experience of his parents splitting up was unsettling at the time he now feels as though it has helped him with his role in *Neighbours* because he feels it helps a lot if you can relate to the character being played.

Unlike a lot of Australian youngsters, Ashley likes spending a lot of money on expensive clothes. Most Australian teenagers are less clothes-conscious than their British counterparts.

Mummy's Boy?

Ashley Paske

'Maybe Matt is a little bit too Ashley Paske...!'

Erinsborough

While Maggie Dence says she is not superstitious she doesn't, however, like crossing people on stairs. But as the new headmistress of Erinsborough High that is something she is going to have to get used to.

While she plays her role of Dorothy Burke with such school-marmly authority she claims she is nothing like the character and could never see herself in the same role in real life.

Born and educated in Sydney, Maggie still lives in a thirties-style bungalow in the city and is still in love with its beautiful harbour.

Away from *Neighbours* she enjoys relaxing by reading or listening to music; ranging from classical to rock 'n' roll. But she admits to having a soft spot for the tones of Frank Sinatra.

At school Maggie was only interested in art, and hated maths. It was her love of art that eventually took her via the theatre to *Neighbours* when approached by Grundy.

Like her fellow cast members she feels the atmosphere on the set is warm and friendly and also believes the programme is similar to parts of suburban life in Melbourne.

Maggie's friends and family have been very supportive of her work throughout her career, not just since she joined *Neighbours* but, inevitably, the demands of work mean she sometimes sees less of her family and friends than she would like.

The kids of Erinsborough occasionally need disciplining and Dorothy Burke was not popular when she became headmistress of Erinsborough High.

Maggie Dence

'If I could have been anybody in history I would have liked to have been Captain Cook.'

AUSTRALIA

AUSTRALIA

*S*PORTING LIFE

■ Australia has produced some great surfing champions, Mark Salisbury is one of the latest.

Australians take their sport seriously and when it comes to playing the old country there is nothing sweeter than a victory.

■ Australia's cricket captain Allan Border at the wicket against India.

Like England, Australia's summer sport is cricket. But unlike England, they seem to win test matches these days, under the leadership of Allan Border, the man who Ian Smith (Harold

DOWN UNDER

Bishop) believes to have been one of Australia's finest ambassadors in recent years.

The national winter game is Australian Rules Football, known simply as Aussie Rules. A fast and physical game played with a rugby-type ball, it appears to have no rules to the uninitiated ... but it does!

Rugby league is popular in Queensland and New South Wales but the whole nation was aware of the 'Roos' success over Great Britain in 1990. And that would have pleased Ian Williams (Adam Willis) a keen rugby fan.

The beaches and climate make surfing a popular participation sport. And the weather is ideal for golf as many hopefuls dream of becoming Australia's next Greg Norman.

However, the biggest Australian sporting event is the Melbourne Cup horse race at Flemington Park on the first Tuesday of November. It is the equivalent of the Epsom Derby and Melbourne comes to a standstill on Cup day. They certainly take their sport seriously in Australia.

■ Action from the Aussie Rules 'Cup Final', the Victoria Football League Grand final, between Hawthorn and Carlton.

21

Kristian Schmid

'I hope that because of Neighbours, people have a broader view of Australia.'

'tarry-Eyed Lovers

Other 16-year-old boys were green with envy when Todd had that first kiss with Melissa.

Jade Amenta

Jade Amenta was the lucky girl who had to kiss Todd, sending twinges of jealousy through the hearts of thousands of teenage girl fans of *Neighbours*.

Sixteen-year-old Melissa was Todd's first true love but, even though they were acting, her real-life boy friend was not too happy about the passionate scenes. Fortunately for the boy friend, the scriptwriter decided to cut down on the passion.

But Jade's on screen romances regularly carry over into her real life because the two questions most often asked of her when she bumps into fans are: 'How's Todd?' and 'Is Josh a good kisser?'

Jade is a Taurean and is very much like her star sign; she is stubborn, and loves money and food, particularly pasta and garlicky sauces. As to comparing her with Melissa: 'We're not at all similar,' says Jade. 'She's too grown up and sensible.'

Both Jade and Kristian had common likes during their schooldays. Jade enjoyed drama and catering, while Kristian's favourite subjects were drama and . . . lunch-time. But is was fortunate for him that he wasn't out at lunch when casting director for *Neighbours* auditioned for 'someone with spiky hair' at his school otherwise he may have missed out on the role of Todd. And that would have meant missing that first kiss with Melissa.

But, fortunately for his many fans, he was around when the casting director arrived and 16-year-old Kristian is now one of the series' heart-throbs.

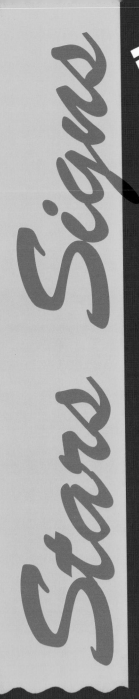

Stars Signs

Anne Haddy: Interest in art and music and a loving nature are typical Libran traits. It is therefore no surprise to learn that Anne was born under this sign. Beauty and elegance are other Libran features which typify Anne.

Scorpio

Stefan Dennis: Stefan enjoys a wide variety of sports and is successful in business. These are typical attributes of the Scorpio who are supposed to have energy and drive.

Virgo

Paul Keane: With the ruling planet of Mercury in his star sign Paul is supposed to be able to communicate, be intelligent and have a sharp wit. Des certainly fits into that category.

Aquarius

Maggie Dence: Ruled by the planet Uranus, Aquarians show independence and inventiveness. While Maggie believes she has some Aquarian traits she doesn't think Dorothy is anything like an Aquarian.

Taurus

Miranda Fryer: Most Taurians have a loving nature and an interest in arts and music. That fits Miranda to a tee. They can also be stubborn and temperamental . . . her mum will agree.

Capricorn

Ben Geurens: Capricorns have great foresight, are hardworking and learn from experience. Ben doesn't read his stars, but if he fits that description then he should have a long and successful career in acting.

Cancer

Ashley Paske: Ruled by the Moon, Cancerians are sensitive and prone to emotional moods. That describes Matt. But they are also romantics, so watch out girls!

Pisces

Linda Hartley: Linda has the rich imagination with which Pisceans are endowed. Although not too practical, Pisceans are given to inspiration and these traits have helped Linda to become the successful actress she is today.

PUZZLE PAGE

CROSSWORD

Crossword grid (answers filled in):

Row 1: H A R O L D | M A N G E L
Row 7: L U M P | N I C K ... P L O T
Row 11: R O N Y | S T E F A N
Row 14/15: A M E L I A
Row 18: S L I P
Row 19: R A M S
Row 21: T W I N | I R O N
Row 23/24: A S H L E Y

ACROSS

1 Mr Bishop (6)
3 Joe . . . (6)
7 Some of the emotional scenes in *Neighbours* brings one of these to your throat (4)
9 Boy taken into Helen's care (4)
10 One of just many intriguing ones in *Neighbours* each week (4)
11 Jim and Bev's baby (4)
12 (and 2 down) Plays the part of Paul (6,6)
15 . . . Frid plays Cody Willis (6)
18 Too many beers in the Waterhole may cause you to do this? (4)
19 Ramsay without the AY (4)
21 Christina is one of these (4)
22 Australia is one of the world's biggest producers of this metal (4)
23 Richard . . . plays the part of Ryan McLachlan (6)
24 On set he is Matt but in real life he is . . .? (6)

WHO AM I?

From the following clues work out which character we are talking about.

1 The first letter of name is in HEAT but not in FIRE.
2 The second is in BEACH but not in SAND.
3 The third is in LIGHT but not in DARK.
4 The fourth is in NEIGHBOURS and also in FRIENDS.
5 The fifth and last is in NEAR but not in FAR.

1 The first letter of my name is in MUM but not in DAD.
2 The second is in DAUGHTER but not in SON.
3 The third is in LONDON but not in MELBOURNE.
4 The fourth is in GREAT BRITAIN but not in AUSTRALIA.
5 The fifth and last is in EVENING but not in MORNING.

Answers on page 6

26

WHERE?

A series of puzzles to test your knowledge of the characters, actors and events of *Neighbours*.

DOWN

1 Matt's mother (6)
2 see 13 across
4 Did two kangaroos, two koalas, two possums, and two wallabies go in it with the other animals? (3)
5 Paul's estranged wife (4)
6 Does Mark have to be 'small' to play Joe? (6)
8 Marsupial who nearly got Harold into bother in the Coffee Shop (6)
13 These girls share the same surname as a 1970s pop duo (6)
14 City in Northern Australia (6)
16 Jade . . . (6)
17 Melbourne's rival city (6)
20 Headmaster at Erinsborough High (4)
21 Number of *Neighbours* showings each day! (3)

From the clues below fill in the Neighbours grid. One letter from each answer is already given.

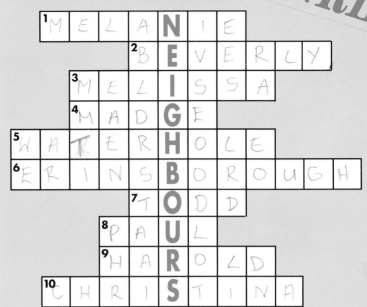

GRID

1 MELANIE
2 BEVERLY
3 MELISSA
4 MADGE
5 WATERHOLE
6 ERINSBOROUGH
7 TODD
8 PAUL
9 HAROLD
10 CHRISTINA

CLUES

1 This character might have a funny laugh but she's not bad at poker
2 She used to look after her nephew and niece
3 In real life she's Jade
4 This lady took self-defence lessons after being mugged
5 The only place to go if you want a 'tinny'
6 Do they say "High" at this school
7 Stayed to continue his education while his sister went to live with their mother
8 Lassiter's whizz kid!
9 Tricked his son-in-law into doing voluntary work at the Church
10 The oldest twin by nine minutes

RELATIVES

1 What is Harold's granddaughter's name? SKY
2 What relation is Todd to Beverly? NEPHEW
3 Who is Madge's step-daughter? KERRY
4 What is the name of Helen's oldest grandson? PAUL
5 What are the twins names? CAROLINE & CHRISTINA

JOBS

1 Who used to be a bank manager? DEZ
2 Who runs Home James? HELEN
3 Where does Madge work? WATERHOLE
4 Whose son went to New Zealand to become a radio presenter? MADGE'S
5 Who is Paul's secretary? MELANIE

AND THEN THERE WERE 4

Name the four characters who survive from the very first episode of *Neighbours*?
MADGE
DEZ
JIM

ALL MIXED UP

Five *Neighbours* characters have got their names in a tangle. Can you sort them out?

1 DAN TODDLERS
2 RIBS JINMOON
3 CLARK SEED
4 SPIKY HOBS
5 BRAVE MARY SHELL

27

Not known for their moderation — INXS.

SUN & SURF &

Getting down to business — Men at Work.

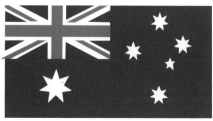

AUSTRALIA

AUSTRALIA

Since the day that Rolf Harris took 'Tie Me Kangaroo Down Sport' into the British hit parade in 1960 there has been a succession of Australians who have made an impact on the British and US charts.

Thanks to the success of *Grease* and *Xanadu*, Australia-born **Olivia Newton-John** has earned herself a rightful place amongst the superstars of the pop business. In 1974 '*Honestly I Love You*' took her to the top of the US charts. She had seven more number ones in the States and four in Britain.

INXS have been one of Oz's top groups in the last couple of years. They

Olivia — Seventies' 'Neutron Bomb'.

ROCK 'N' ROLL

Plugged in — AC/DC's lead guitarist Angus Young.

were formed in Sydney in 1977 as the Farriss brothers. In 1988 lead singer Michael Hutchence was voted 'Hunkiest Pop Star in United States'. Their biggest hit was '*Need You Tonight*' which topped the US charts and reached number two in Britain.

AC/DC are another group formed in Sydney in the mid-Seventies. Lead singer Bon Scott died tragically in 1980 and the group was reformed with English-born Brian Johnson as the new lead singer. That same year they had their first number one '*Back in the Black*'.

Men at Work are a Melbourne group formed in 1979 by Scottish-born Colin Hay (vocals) and Ron Strykert (guitar). They came to the fore in 1982 when their debut LP '*Business as Usual*' spent 15 weeks at No. 1 in the US album charts. They have since had many more single and LP successes.

29

Harold and Madge with coffee-shop rival Eddie Buckingham.

The residents of Ramsay Street have encountered many ups and downs since they first appeared on our television screens in October 1986.

Because the coffee shop is one of the meeting places for the residents of Ramsay Street it is therefore understandable that many of the ups and downs of *Neighbours* occur there.

But the coffee shop was nearly closed down by the health inspector after it was reported there was a possum on the premises. However, it turned out to be one that Bronwyn was looking after and fortunately the closure was averted.

When he noticed an upward trend in custom Harold wondered why. But all was revealed when he found out there were signs advertising half-price meals outside the shop. But who put them there? All was revealed when Joe owned up to the signs as part of the on-going feud between him and his father-in-law. Harold got his own

Street

back by arranging work for Joe in the church hall repairing the seats. Joe thought Harold had let bygones-be-bygones until he found out he wasn't getting paid for the job.

Melanie arrived in Ramsey Street like a breath of fresh air, even if she brought that dreadful laugh of hers with her. When she moved in with Des she was just what he needed for some motivation. But when she helped him to get his job in the stockbrokers she was over enthusiastic and compiled an exaggerated resumé for him after his own CV seemed rather dull. He got the job, and it subsequently resulted in him meeting his new fiancée Fiona.

A bit of a busybody, Melanie is,

> **Clarrie McLachlan with his trusty canine friend Rosie.**

nevertheless, kind and always on hand to help people. She manages to steer clear of some nasty scrapes as she did when writing letters to 'Dear George' about Ramsay Street residents' problems.

After Paul, Caroline, Matt and some record shop customers gave Melanie the impression she had hidden singing talents she turned to Harold for singing lessons. But he soon realised he had a hopeless case on his hands. ▶

6 PAGE

SPECIAL

> **Melanie with that often seen 'I'm sorry Des' look on her face.**

Madge clearly shows what she thinks of Melanie's singing!

▶ Melanie's singing went on late into the night and it was only after she overheard some cruel jokes about her voice that she eventually decided to end her ambitions to become a singer ... much to the delight of Harold and many others.

Harold has had his own share of ups and downs without having the added problem of Melanie's voice, and his battle with Madge over his candidature for the Erinsborough Council caused a rift between the two.

Harold was delighted to be asked to stand as councillor, but Madge wasn't too happy when she discovered that if he was elected he wouldn't fight to stop the demolition of the Jack Ramsay fountain. So, Madge decided to stand in opposition and war was declared in the Bishop household. However, the family dis-

The 'Belle of the Ball', Melanie with her escort Matt.

Joe, Helen and Madge wait while Harold phones for the election result.

pute was resolved quickly, as they normally are when Harold and Madge fall out, when Harold withdrew his nomination after finding out that his sponsors, the Erinsborough Business Council, were sponsoring another candidate and were also involved in a shady land deal. As a result, Harold gave Madge his full support and went to the *Erinsborough News* with details of the scandal and Madge was duly elected.

'Neighbours *is* relatable to all western countries.'

Harold and Madge's isn't the only Ramsay Street marriage to have its ups and downs. Jim and Beverly have had many traumas over the years and after bringing up Jim's children, and Bev's nephew and niece, they were awarded the guardianship of baby Rhys who was left with Beverly by his young mother.

They were just starting to enjoy the taste of new parenthood when Rhys was taken from them to be adopted. The combination of this and a recent miscarriage caused Beverly to throw herself deeply into her medical practice.

A strain on their marriage resulted in Bev moving to live at the surgery, taking Todd with her. He has also had his share of problems with the opposite sex and has kept us guessing about his on-off relationships with Melissa and Cody. And his befriending of Boof nearly got him into very deep trouble when they were accused of stealing a carburettor for Todd's trail bike. Luckily, Todd received only a court warning.

Happily all is well in the Robinson ▶

(Above) The strain on their marriage is clearly shown in the face of Jim and Bev. (Below) Todd contemplating his love life.

household again. Todd is rid of Boof, while Jim and Beverly are settled down and Bev is expecting a much wanted baby.

But the big romantic occasion of the year was the wedding of Kerry and Joe which took place in the Butterfly House of the local zoo. Kerry looked lovely in her Indian-style outfit, while Joe also dressed up for the occasion and swapped his shorts for a suit.

But it is not only the people of Ramsay Street who have had their ups and downs. Bouncer was delighted when Clarrie McLachlan, Dorothy's father, arrived with his old blue cattle dog Rosie. The two of them went missing overnight and after searching for them Joe and Kerry checked at the dog pound and found Rosie, but there was no sign of Bouncer. However, Rosie led them to the quarry where Bouncer was trapped. He was hungry but unhurt and taken home.

Practical joker Joe clowning on his wedding day at the Butterfly House.

6 PAGE

SPECIAL

Linda Hartley

'I've never been to England but I can feel it buzzing. I can't wait to see it.'

Lucky Couple

Joe is the joker and quick-tempered one of the Mangel household. But fortunately Kerry is the calming influence.

Mark Little started his acting career in school plays when he lived in Queensland. He reckons that Joe's down-to-earth approach, sense of humour, and quick temper is nothing like his own personality and he has to work hard to create Joe's character.

Linda was educated at Watsonia South Primary and then McLeod High but, unlike Mark, she didn't have early ambitions to be an actress, though she took up dancing at six. However, when she was 12 she got the lead role in a mini-series and after working for the Grundy Organisation got the part of Kerry after successfully coming through the screen test.

Linda finds it very difficult to relax and has to be doing something all the time. She puts that down to the nature of the acting profession, but she is slowly learning how to switch off in between performances. Gardening is one of her favourite pastimes.

The success that *Neighbours* has brought Mark and Linda hasn't changed either of them. Both carry on their lives the way they always have but, of course, there is the adulation from fans. Mark handles them 'with a smile' while Linda likes being thanked for doing a nice job because, as she says: 'There's not too many industries where that happens.'

Linda believes the success of *Neighbours* is because people like the sun, the friendly atmosphere of suburban Melbourne, and people wearing colourful clothes. *Neighbours* offers that, but how does the programme truly reflect suburban Melbourne? 'I think it reflects it very well,' says Linda. 'Not at all,' says Mark. Oh well! That's Joe and Kerry for you.

Mark Little

How well do

A general knowledge quiz to see how much you know about the country in which the residents of Ramsay Street live.

1 Give the two names Barry Humphries is better known as? (One point for each).
2 What is the capital of Australia?
3 Neighbours is set in Melbourne. But in which state is Melbourne?
4 Where is Australia's famous Opera House?
5 What is the name of the rock which is virtually in the centre of Australia?

6 Six *what* appear on the Australian flag?
7 What is the name of the famous beach close to Sydney?
8 Which Australian sportsman is better known as 'The Great White Shark'?
9 Who or what are Australians talking about when they mention 'Alice'?

Aussie slang

Some slang words that you may come across in Ramsay Street when listening to Strine . . . that's slang for the Australian language!

BUSH . . . Countryside, away from the city
COBBER . . . Mate
COMBI . . . Caravanette/ Camper Van
DELI . . . Delicatessen

DUNNY . . . Outhouse/ Outside toilet
FAIR GO! . . . Give us a break
GOOD ON YER . . . W done
HOON . . . Idiot, hoolig

ABO . . . Aboriginal
BEAUT . . . Great/Fantastic
BLUDGER . . . Lazy person who won't work
BONZER . . . Great!

DINKUM/FAIR DINKUM . . . Honest, genuine, really?
DRONGO . . . Worthless person
DUCO . . . Car paint

LOLLIES . . . Sweets, ca
LURK . . . A scheme
MOZZIES . . . Mosquito
OCKER . . . A basic dow to-earth Australian

you know Australia?

15 Who discovered Australia in 1770? (Clue: also the person Dorothy Burke would most like to have been in history!)
16 What is the unit of currency in Australia, the dollar or the pound?
17 Who played the part of Crocodile Dundee?
18 What famous sporting trophy did the Australians take from the Americans in 1983 after 113 years of American domination?
19 How is Pin-Oak Court, Melbourne, better known?
20 What is the name of the large island off the south coast of Australia?

10 What sport do Carlton, Essendon and Collingwood play?
11 Once famous for the hit record '*Tie Me Kangaroo Down Sport*', this Australian is now better known as an artist. Who is he?
12 What is the name of Australia's major airline?
13 As the plane flies, is it approximately (*a*) 15,673 (*b*) 17,008 or (*c*) 19,239 kilometres from London to Sydney?
14 The largest coral formation in the world is located off the east coast of Australia. What is it called?

OFF-SIDER . . Assistant
POM . . . English person
RATBAG . . . A term of friendly abuse
RAPT . . . Delighted
RIPPER . . . Good

SNAGS . . . Sausages
SURFIES . . . People who go surfboarding
TINNY . . . Can of beer
TOO RIGHT! . . . Absolutely! Definitely!

. . . Kangaroo
ANGERS . . . ndwiches
E'LL BE RIGHT . . . worries/no problem
OOT THROUGH . . . e quickly
KIE . . . Day off work ill
KE-O . . . Tea break

TUCKER . . . Food
UNI . . . University
UTE . . . Pick up truck (short for Utility)
WAG . . . To skip school

SEE HOW GOOD *YOU* ARE ON AUSTRALIAN SLANG?

■ Occupations
What do you think the following all do for a living?
(**a**) Journo   (**b**) Milko
(**c**) Postie   (**d**) Wharfie
(**e**) Woolgrower

■ Around Ramsay Street
What do you think the following are slang for (all of which are likely to be found in Ramsay Street)
(**a**) Barbie   (**b**) Mayo
(**c**) Relo   (**d**) Sheila
(**e**) Stickybeak

Answers on page 61

39

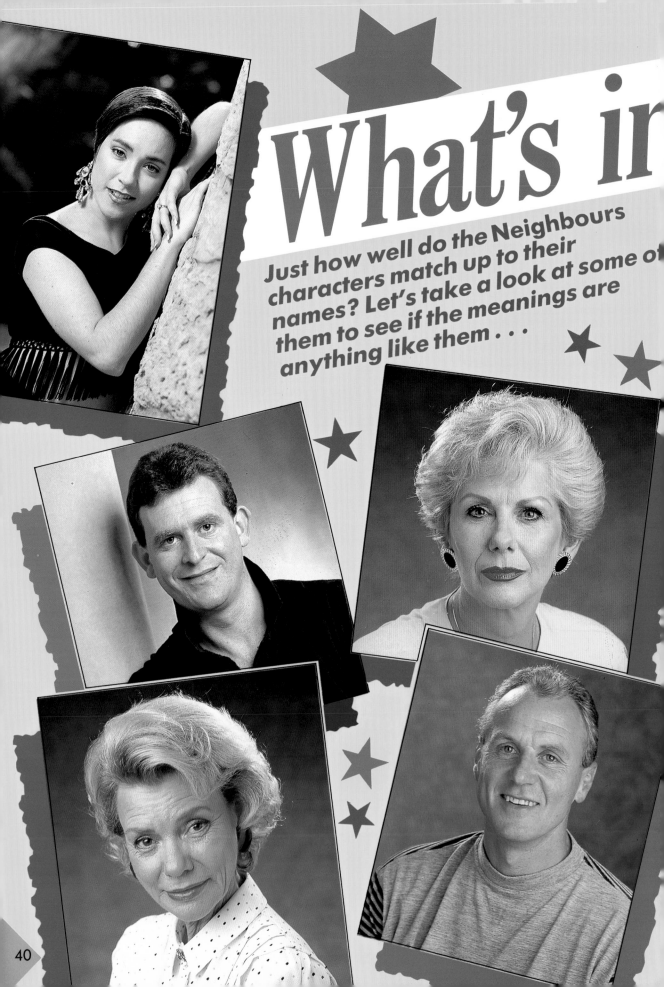

What's in

Just how well do the Neighbours characters match up to their names? Let's take a look at some of them to see if the meanings are anything like them . . .

a Name?

Madge (**Bishop**) is a pet name for Margaret. Margaret is a Greek word meaning *pearl* and I'm sure Harold would agree that Madge is his pearl . . . well, most of the time!

Helen (**Daniels**) is also a Greek name meaning *the bright one* which is also very relevant because Helen brings so much brightness and happiness into people's lives in Ramsay Street.

Jim (**Robinson**) on the other hand does not match up to the meaning of his name which is the English form of the Hebrew name Jacob, meaning *follower*. But Jim is no follower, he is invariably at the thick of the action in Ramsay Street.

Kerry (**Bishop**) is supposed to be *the dark one*, if you look at the Gaelic translation of her name. But she's far from being a dark horse, although it is a description of the colour of Kerry's hair.

Des (**Clarke**) is also a Gaelic derivation from the name Desmond meaning *Man from South Munster*. Unless he was once seen with a bolt through his neck or has Irish connections then I'm afraid his name just doesn't match up.

On the other hand, if anybody is appropriately named it is **Harold** (**Bishop**) Harold comes from the German name meaning *leader of the army* . . . that's Harold. If there's any organising to be done, he's the one for the job.

Beverly (**Robinson**) might get a clue from her name if she ever considers quitting her medical practice. Beverly is an English name meaning *meadow of the beaver*, so maybe she could go in for caring about animals and become a vet.

Finally **Melissa** (**Jarrett**), is the Greek name for *bee*, and she certainly has the young male residents of Ramsey Street buzzing.

The Twins –

When the Alessi twins moved into Ramsay Street they caused confusion all round, and not least to Paul.

Christina and Caroline Alessi's arrival in Ramsay Street brought glamour to Erinsborough. But it also brought a considerable amount of confusion.

The 22-year-old identical twins certainly confused Paul and had the viewers just wondering who was who at times. To put the record straight – Gillian (the 'G' is a hard 'G' as in golf) Blakeney plays Caroline, while Gayle is Christina. Being so alike poses problems, not just for Paul, even the girls' parents get them mixed up when watching them in *Neighbours*.

Born and educated in Brisbane the twins had acting in their blood from an early age. They first appeared in school plays, and when they were nine they appeared in a national television commercial for cornflakes. But their mother thought schoolwork was more important and their acting days seemed to be over. When they left school the two girls followed other careers. But a chance meeting between Gillian and a TV director who remembered the cornflake advert resulted in them being offered a job hosting a children's series called *Wombat*. After three years they landed their parts in *Neighbours* after writing to Grundy.

The twins are very much alike; both feel they are maternal, which is consistent with their star sign Cancer. Neither likes hot weather, their favourite drink is water, and they both dislike grumpy people. They have similar tastes in music and are looking forward to furthering their own musical careers.

Seeing Double

Gayle & Gillian Blakeney

'If I could play any other character in Neighbours it would be Melanie; I'd love to be a little wacky!'
Gayle

AUSTRALIA

■ The animal that is synonym with Australia — the kangaro This is the red kangaroo.

AUSTRALIA'S W

■ Koalas, but don't be fooled by their 'cuddly' looks.

Australian animals that elsewhere can only be seen in zoos or wildlife parks.

■ (Above) Another of Australia's marsupials, the Wombat. (Below) The duck-billed platypus, an unusual looking character. He appears to be a cross between a hamster and a duck. (Bottom) Australia's wild dog, the dingo, seen with a new addition.

LD NEIGHBOURS

Ask most people to name two things Australian and after *Neighbours* it is a good bet the other will be the **kangaroo**.

The 'roo' is a marsupial that carries its young, the joey, in its pouch. It has large back legs for hopping and the larger roos can jump 9ft (3m) in a single leap. There are many species and the **wallaby** is one example of the smaller variety.

The **koala** may appear to be a cuddly bear-like animal but don't be fooled; he is not particularly nice and has a short temper. Found in Eastern Australia he loves eating eucalyptus leaves. He is usually incorrectly called a koala bear.

Another marsupial is the **wombat** which is also bear-like with a round body and small tail. Like the koala it has a large padded nose.

You would have to go a long way to find a nicer dog than *Neighbours'* Bouncer, but the wild **dingo** is much feared and attacks kangaroos, sheep and rabbits. A descendant of the domestic dog, it is reddish-brown but cannot bark.

The **duck-billed platypus** is a most unusual looking animal. A native of Eastern Australia, it is semi-aquatic and resembles a large hamster but with four webbed feet and a duck's bill.

And finally, the **possum**. Remember the one that got loose in the coffee shop and nearly got Harold into trouble?

Ramsay Street?

J im and Beverly are the pillars of Ramsay Street society, but the last twelve months have brought them their fair share of traumatic moments and, as quality performers have brought realism to their roles.

Both Alan Dale and Shaunna O'Grady are experienced actors and while Shaunna fully appreciates the insecurity of the acting profession she still wants to carry on performing as long as she can. Strangely, although she attended drama school after finishing High School in Sydney she didn't intend acting professionally. But when the chance to play Bev came along she jumped at it because: 'Beverly came across as a strong professional woman who combined her career with her family life' and that appealed to Shaunna.

Alan's character is similar; a career-minded person fully appreciative of the family unit. Alan, however, hasn't been too settled on the home front ... he has lived in 35 different homes. But New Zealand born Alan is now firmly settled in a Melbourne beach house with his new wife Tracey, their poodle Terry, cat Roon, and a canary called Bird!

He keeps himself trim by swimming, sailboarding, playing golf and tennis. Like Jim, Alan is level headed. He vows that success hasn't changed him, despite: 'Having a bit more money now'. But he feels that his success has meant a tougher life for his two sons from a previous marriage. But if they have Alan's character then they shouldn't have too many problems.

Two of the senior members of the Neighbours cast, Alan Dale and Shaunna O'Grady create the ideal couple.

Alan Da

Mature Couple

Shaunna O'Grady

'People who patronise soaps don't usually watch them.'

Anne Haddy

'Helen seems very balanced ...until she's unbalanced.'

# of Ramsay Street

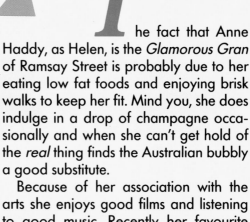

> When all is not going well it's nice to know there is a shoulder to lean on, and Grans normally fit that role. Helen Daniels is the perfect Gran.

The fact that Anne Haddy, as Helen, is the *Glamorous Gran* of Ramsay Street is probably due to her eating low fat foods and enjoying brisk walks to keep her fit. Mind you, she does indulge in a drop of champagne occasionally and when she can't get hold of the *real* thing finds the Australian bubbly a good substitute.

Because of her association with the arts she enjoys good films and listening to good music. Recently her favourite films have been Mel Gibson's *Hamlet* and Kenneth Branagh's *Henry V.* And on the music scene she thoroughly enjoyed Carreras, Domingo, and Pavarotti in concert; as did many other people.

Anne became interested in acting while at school in Adelaide but didn't go to drama school because, as she says: 'There weren't any here at the time.' She was good at English and drama at school and if her acting career hadn't been successful she could possibly have fallen back on her shorthand and typing skills which she picked up in her school days.

She was invited to appear in *Neighbours* by the producers and is one of the few *Neighbours* actors who remembers their first words. They were: 'Jim, would you like a cup of tea?'

If she could play the part of any other *Neighbours* character Anne would like to be Bouncer. Perhaps she thinks being a dog is less arduous than being a Gran?

Anne feels as though she is only slightly similar to Helen. However, it would appear that their sense of humour is similar.

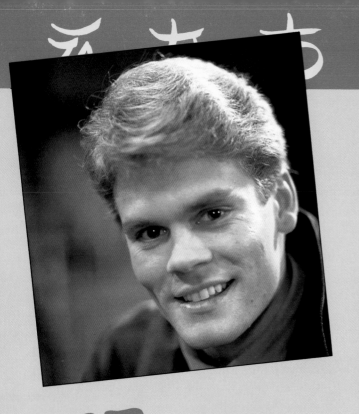

CHINESE

Horoscopes

According to legend, Buddha invited all the animals in his Kingdom to a celebration but only twelve turned up and he named a year after each one. The twelve were: Cat, Dog, Dragon, Goat, Horse, Monkey, Ox, Pig, Rat, Rooster, Snake and Tiger. The twelve signs of the Chinese Zodiac are named after these animals, just like the Western Zodiac is named Pisces, Aries, Libra, etc. It is said that if you were born under one of these signs you will inherit its characteristics.

The Chinese New Year does not start on 1 January, in fact, the start of the New Year changes every year. The 1991 New Year was on 15 February and is the year of the Goat. While the 1992 New Year starts on 4 February and will be the year of the Monkey.

Let's look at some Neighbours actors and find out what they are in the Chinese Zodiac.

Ian Williams was born on 30 April 1968 which was the year of the **Monkey**. Monkeys are inquisitive, lovable and friendly. They like to do a job well and are able to improvise. Assets which will help Ian's acting career. However, on the minus side they can tend to be silly and talk a lot. But, in his profession, that must surely be a plus for Ian.

If you combine Ian's Eastern and Western signs he is a Taurus/Monkey and other famous Taurus/Monkeys include champion boxer Sugar Ray Leonard, Leonardo da Vinci and Pope John Paul II.

Lucinda Cowden doesn't follow the Chinese stars but is aware that she is a **Snake**; 'So watch out!' she says. The Snake sign is one of wisdom and Snakes are always keeping their minds active and planning things . . . that's Melanie! They also think deeply about decisions and also act upon their own intuition. Being born on 24 April 1965 Lucinda is a Taurus/Snake and she shares those dual horoscopes with two very famous people from her own profession; Henry Fonda and Audrey Hepburn.

Anne Haddy is a **Horse** and because of it she calls her car (a Suzuki Vitara) *Horse*. Horses can be bad tempered and rebellious; that's not Helen. But they can also be charming and popular people; that's more like her. They enjoy socialising and like to be the centre of attention and the learning of new skills come easy to the Horse. Funny man Rowan Atkinson is a fellow horse and actress Rita Hayworth is a Libra/Horse like Anne.

Alan Dale doesn't follow the Chinese horoscopes but he may be interested to know that he is a **Pig** . . . They are hardworking, always ready to understand and help others and are honest and sociable. The Duchess of York is also a Pig. And being a Taurus/Pig Alan shares the dual sign with Fred Astaire, Oliver Cromwell and empire builder William Randolph Hearst.

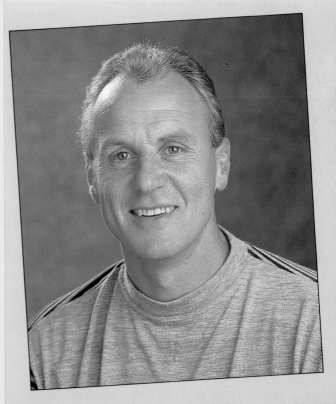

The High-Flyers

Paul Keane

Des and Paul are the two high-flying executives of Ramsay Street ...even if Des acquired his current position with a little help from Melanie.

For Paul Keane, relaxation means playing drums (even if it's not too relaxing for *his* neighbours), reading, and listening to music. He has a varied musical taste but likes Broderick Smith, Bruce Springstein and the Australian band Cold Chisel.

When he auditioned for the part of Des he was attracted by scope for humour, drama and realism the part offered, and there has been plenty of those characteristics in the role. He appreciates how hard everyone works to make the series as realistic as possible.

Unlike Paul Keane, Stefan Dennis is an 'action man' and likes to spend his spare time partaking in a variety of sports, ranging from water-skiing, surfing, cycling, motor cycling, skating and archery. Perhaps surprisingly he doesn't watch a lot of sport.

He is a very adventurous person, which explains why Neil Armstrong is one of the men in history he would liked to have been.

When recording permits, Stefan likes to get as far away from the 'rat race' as possible and he has even found time to visit Britain in his time off and being an outdoor type found the Scottish Highlands a great place to be. He also particularly liked Bath.

Like Paul Keane, Stefan doesn't think his character is similar to his own personality but he enjoys the part of Paul Robinson because of the variety of the role.

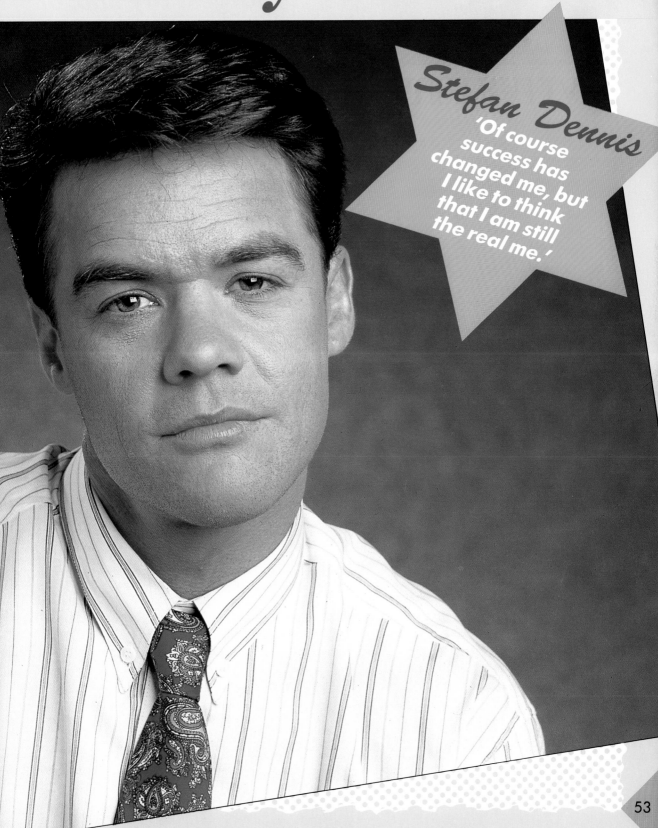

Stefan Dennis

'Of course success has changed me, but I like to think that I am still the real me.'

AUSTRALIA

AUSTRALIA

Although not the capital of Australia, Melbourne is the country's second largest city and, of course, is where Neighbours *is set.*

To most of us Melbourne (that's Mel*burn*, not Mel*born*) is that far-away place that is the home of *Neighbours*, but there is a lot more going on beyond the confines of *Ramsay Street* in Australia's second city.

Melbourne has a population of nearly three million and is situated on the River Yarra at the head of Port Phillip Bay. It is the state capital of Victoria and was founded in 1835 and named after the former British Prime Minister Lord Melbourne. Between 1901 and 1927 it was the capital of Australia.

The city has two airports, two cathedrals, and three universities; the first was opened in 1855 and the last in 1964. There is also an extensive railway system

THE MAGIC OF

The dragon boat race which forms part of the annual Moomba festival.

MELBOURNE

in Melbourne as well as an underground and tram system.

It is the largest cargo port in Australia and major industries include shipbuilding, engineering, chemicals, electronics, clothing and textile manufacture.

On a sporting front Melbourne is very famous. The Melbourne Cricket Ground was the scene of the very first Test Match in 1877, and the Melbourne Cup horse race, like the English Derby, is one of the great social events of the year.

Sporting events, along with street parades and cultural activities, form part of the 10-day long 'Moomba' carnival at the beginning of March each year.

■ The Yarra dominates much of Melbourne's geography and this view of it includes Victoria Dock.

Ian Smith

"Who do I like most?" is the question most frequently asked of me.'

nd the Chorister

Despite the occasional ups and downs, Madge and Harold are a well matched couple. But how much alike are they in real life?

Anne Charleston

Madge and Harold have been described as the 'Odd Couple' of *Neighbours*. It is clear to see why at times, but in real life Anne Charleston and Ian Smith have a lot in common and are far from the 'Odd Couple'.

They have many mutual likes. They both enjoy seafood and when it comes to dress, they both enjoy nothing more than the casual look, although Anne does enjoy donning an evening gown every so often.

Melbourne is the favourite city of both Anne and Ian. They were both born and educated in the city and it is 'home'; the place they both enjoy returning to after spreading their wings further afield. They have both been to England and thoroughly enjoyed the history of the country, even if they didn't think much of the weather. Ian also liked the people while Anne, although not disliking them, found the open spaces of the countryside more appealing. She particularly liked the Brighton area, and the Sussex resort is her favourite English city. Ian's favourite is the Roman city of York.

Prior to becoming an actor Ian wanted to be a singer and enjoys all types of music except heavy metal. Anne's taste is more classical, but her favourite record of the last year was 'Home' by Hothouse Flowers. Anne has other musical connections because her son is a rock singer. He has her total support because, as she says: 'I will appreciate being kept in my old age.'

Ramsay Street's

Ian Williams has done a lot of moving around but has now got his feet firmly on the ground since landing the part of Adam Willis in *Neighbours*.

Ian was born at Vancouver Island, Canada, and lived in the United States before the family moved to Australia. Since arriving in Oz he has lived in Canberra, Darwin and Brisbane, where his family still resides.

After attending many different schools, Ian went to drama college in 1985 and it was after appearing in another Grundy production, *Bony*, that he was invited to play the part of Adam in *Neighbours*.

The part appeals to Ian because it is a flexible role; he is not tied down and Adam's humour always keeps him fired-up. Ian, however, could not see himself working in medicine in real life; he's happy acting and wants to carry on doing that for a long time.

A lover of the outdoors Ian lives in an open unit in South Yarra. But to look at his list of pets you would think he lived in a zoo. He has two dogs, 'Midge' and 'Dak', a goat called 'Goat', a cat called 'Cat', 'Abe' and 'Mary', the peach-faced love birds and various ducks and chooks.

The love of the outdoors means that Ian is a keen sportsman and he enjoys swimming, doing aerobics, and playing touch football. He also enjoys watching sport, either live or from the comfort of his armchair and swimming and rugby league are two of his favourites.

Ian Williams feels as though he is similar to his character in the show. They are both young and love their families. But he's not too impressed with Adam's naïvety.

Flying Doctor

Ian Williams

'If I didn't play Adam I would like to be Joe, I like his attitude to life and he's lot's of fun.'

FAN CLUB *Special*

For those who can't get enough of the Land of Oz . . .

NEIGHBOURS is a TV series which has inspired total devotion. For some people two episodes a day just isn't enough. If you feel that way, then the *Neighbours* official fan club is the ideal solution for you too. As well as providing you with an introductory package of Aussie memorabilia, they'll keep you informed of what's going on in Erinsborough with the regular *Ramsay Street News*.

If you wish to join the Neighbours Fan Club please send a stamped-addressed envelope to The Neighbours Fan Club, P.O. Box 136, Watford, Herts WD2 4ND.

ANSWERS
Puzzle Page Pages 26 and 27

Crossword Solution

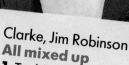

1 H	A	R	O	L	D		3 M	A	N	5 G	E	6 L
I			E		R			R		A		I
7 L	U	8 M	P		9 N	I	C	K		I		T
A		O			I			I		10 P	L	O	T
11 R	H	Y	S		S			I		L		E
Y		S			12 S	T	E	F	13 A	N		E
		U					L			S
14 D		15 A	M	E	L	I	16 A			17 S
A			M				M			Y
19 R	A	20 M	S			18 S	W	A	Y		D
W		U				S		T			N
I		21 I		T	W	I	N	22 I	R	O	N
23 N	O	R	T	O	N		24 A	S	H	L	E	Y

Neighbours Grid
1 Melanie **2** Beverly **3** Melissa
4 Madge **5** Waterhole **6** Erinsborough
7 Todd **8** Paul **9** Harold **10** Christina

Who am I? . . . 1
Helen Daniels

Who am I? . . . 2
Madge Bishop

Relatives
1 Sky Bishop **2** Nephew **3** Kerry
Mangel **4** Paul Robinson **5** Christina
and Caroline Alessi

Jobs
1 Des Clarke **2** Helen Daniels **3** The
Waterhole **4** Madge Bishop **5** Melanie
Pearson

And then there were four!
Paul Robinson, Helen Robinson, Des

Clarke, Jim Robinson

All mixed up
1 Todd Landers **2** Jim Robinson **3** Des
Clarke **4** Sky Bishop **5** Beverly Marshall

How Well Do You Know Australia?
Pages 38 and 39
1 Dame Edna Everage or Sir Les
Patterson **2** Canberra **3** Victoria
4 Sydney **5** Ayers Rock **6** Stars
7 Bondi Beach **8** Greg Norman
9 Alice Springs **10** Australian Rules
Football **11** Rolf Harris **12** Qantas
13 (b) 17,008 kilometres **14** Great
Barrier Reef **15** Captain Cook
16 Dollar (Australian dollar) **17** Paul
Hogan **18** America's Cup (Yachting)
19 Ramsay Street **20** Tasmania

Well, How Did You Shape Up?
16-20 There's not a lot we can tell you
about Australia is there?
11-15 A little bit more studying and you
could get into the top bracket next year.
6-10 Lucky for you it's the taking part
and not the winning that's important . . .
0-5 A visit to the library might help,
there are plenty of good books about
Australia!

How Good Were You on Australian Slang?
Occupations
(a) Journalist **(b)** Milkman **(c)** Mailman
(Postman) **(d)** Docker **(e)** Sheep farmer
Around Ramsay Street
(a) Barbecue **(b)** Mayonnaise
(c) Relative **(d)** Woman **(e)** Nosy person